CONTENTS

Published in 2017 by The Rosen Publishing Group, Inc.
29 East 21st Street, New York, NY 10010

Editor: Theresa Morlock
Book Design: Michael Flynn
Interior Layout: Tanya Dellaccio

Photo Credits: Cover MarcelClemens/Shutterstock.com; back cover, p.1 Pitju/Shutterstock.com; p. 5 wavebreakmedia/ Shutterstock.com; p. 6 Maxger/Shutterstock.com; p. 7 (background) Dundanim/Shutterstock.com; p. 7 fluidworkshop/ Shutterstock.com; p. 8 Zzvet/Shutterstock.com; p. 9 Zhang Peng/LightRocket/Getty Images; p. 11 Cathy Hart/ Design Pics/Getty Images; pp. 12, 13 Patrik Bergström/Getty Images; p. 14 https://commons.wikimedia.org/wiki/ File:Ausangate-hillside-MT.jpg; p. 15 Ammit Jack/Shutterstock.com; p. 16 focusstock/Getty Images; p. 17 Courtesy of the New York Public Library; p. 18 Brandi Mueller/Getty Images; p. 19 Marco Saracco/Shutterstock.com; p. 21 (Antarctica) DEA/ M. SANTINI/ De Agostini/Getty Images; p. 21 (inset) https://commons.wikimedia.org/wiki/ File:Endurance_trapped_in_pack_ice.jpg; p. 22 DeAgostini Picture Library/Getty Images.

Library of Congress Cataloging-in-Publication Data

Names: Harris, Irene.
Title: Earth's continents / Irene Harris.
Description: New York : PowerKids Press, 2017. | Series: Spotlight on earth science | Includes index.
Identifiers: ISBN 9781499424966 (pbk.) | ISBN 9781499424997 (library bound) | ISBN 9781499424973 (6 pack)
Subjects: LCSH: Continents--Juvenile literature.
Classification: LCC G133.H297 2017 | DDC 910--d23

Manufactured in China

CPSIA Compliance Information: Batch #BW17PK For further information contact Rosen Publishing, New York, New York at 1-800-237-9932.

CHAPTER ONE

WELCOME TO THE CONTINENTS

Earth's surface is about 70 **percent** water and 30 percent land. The land is broken into huge landmasses called continents. Earth has seven continents—North America, South America, Asia, Europe, Africa, Australia, and Antarctica. Each of the continents has different **climates**, wildlife, geography, and countries.

Earth's landmasses formed billions of years ago. Long ago, geologic events began shaping and building Earth's landforms. Earthquakes, volcanoes, and glaciers created beautiful landscapes. This kind of activity is still affecting the way Earth's continents look. The planet is always changing, and it's important to understand why. That's where earth science comes in.

Earth science is the study of Earth's physical properties. It helps us understand what our planet was like long ago and how it is today. Let's get ready to explore Earth's continents. It will help us learn more about our world!

The study of the continents and what they're made of belongs to a branch of science called earth science.

CHAPTER TWO

ALL ABOUT THE CONTINENTS

Asia is the biggest continent. The next largest is Africa, then North America, South America, Antarctica, and Europe. Australia is the smallest. Altogether, the continents cover 57 million square miles (148 million sq km) of Earth's surface.

Most continental land is found in Earth's Northern Hemisphere, which is the half of the planet above the equator. Antarctica is the only continent that doesn't have any countries.

NORTH AMERICA

EUROPE

ASIA

AFRICA

SOUTH AMERICA

AUSTRALIA

ANTARCTICA

INNER CORE
OUTER CORE
MANTLE
CRUST

Earth is made of four layers—the inner core, outer core, mantle, and crust. The bottom part of the mantle is made of melted rock. The solid upper mantle and crust form a layer called the lithosphere. The lithosphere is broken into plates, which float slowly on top of the melted mantle.

The continents are part of Earth's crust, or outermost layer. On average, the continental crust is about 25 miles (40.2 km) thick. The ocean floors are also part of Earth's crust.

Scientists think Earth's crust and upper **mantle** are broken into huge plates. The continents are part of the plates, which float slowly on a layer of partly melted rock. Millions of years ago, most of the continents were connected as a giant landmass called Pangaea. The movement of Earth's plates caused this continent to break and pieces to drift apart. This idea is called plate tectonics.

CHAPTER THREE

THE AMAZING ASIAN CONTINENT

Asia is the largest continent. It covers 17.2 million square miles (44.5 million sq km). From north to south, it ranges 6,000 miles (9,656 km) from the Arctic regions to the equator. It extends 5,900 miles (9,495 km) from the Pacific Ocean to the east to the Mediterranean Sea to the west. Asia shares a western border with Europe.

Mount Everest in Nepal is Earth's highest mountain.

Asia is not just the largest continent in size, it's also the largest in population. As of 2014, more than 4.4 billion people lived on the continent. They live in countries such as the People's Republic of China, India, Indonesia, Japan, Vietnam, Iran, Afghanistan, Israel, and more.

Scientists generally divide the continent into six types of **environments**. They are mountain systems, **plateaus**, plains, deserts, freshwater environments, and saltwater environments.

The Himalayas, the Tien Shan mountain system, and the Ural Mountains are located in Asia. The Tibetan Plateau, the largest plateau in the world, is part of the continent, too. Many of the world's major rivers are in Asia, including the Ganges, Chang, Tigris, and Euphrates. Because of its large size, different parts of the continent have very different climates. From the cold, frozen lands of Siberia to the wet rain forests of Indonesia, the Asian continent has it all.

CHAPTER FOUR

EXPLORING AFRICA

Africa is the second-largest continent. It's also one of the oldest. Scientists think Africa once had tall mountain ranges, but millions of years of **weathering** and **erosion** wore many of its mountains away. Today, most of the continent is a plateau. However, Africa has the Atlas Mountains and the East African Highlands. Mount Kilimanjaro, which has the tallest peak in Africa, is part of the highlands.

The African continent is divided into eight regions. One is the Sahara desert. It's the world's largest hot desert, covering about 3.3 million square miles (8.5 million sq km), or about 25 percent of Africa. The Sahara features huge sand dunes, plateaus, and plants and animals that have adapted to the extreme temperatures. Most of the people who live in the Sahara live in oases, which are areas with water in the desert.

Africa also has beautiful grasslands, or savannas. They cover almost half of the continent. The famous Serengeti Plain covers 11,583 square miles (30,000 sq km). Elephants, lions, zebras, giraffes, and wildebeests are just some of the animals that live there. Rain forests and a group of large lakes are also found in Africa.

Africa is widely considered the "birthplace of human beings." Scientists think **ancestors** of humans lived on the African continent more than 4 million years ago. Today, more than 1 billion people live in the continent's 54 countries.

CHAPTER FIVE

LEARNING ABOUT NORTH AMERICA

Stretching more than 5,000 miles (8,047 km) from near the North Pole to the equator, North America is the third-largest continent. It makes up the northern half of the land in the Western Hemisphere. North America has 23 countries, including Canada, the United States, and Mexico.

North America is surrounded by the Pacific Ocean, Atlantic Ocean, Arctic Ocean, and the Gulf of Mexico. The continent is home to the five Great Lakes and several major rivers, including the Mississippi River, Missouri River, and Rio Grande.

MEXICO CITY

In North America, the Appalachian Mountains lie in the East and the Rocky Mountains lie in the West. The continent also has low, flat areas, such as the Great Plains and the interior lowlands. The Sierra Madre mountain ranges are in the southern part of the continent, near Mexico.

Europeans landed in North America in the 15th century, but the continent was home to the ancestors of today's Native Americans for thousands of years before that. They may have arrived on the continent using a land bridge from Asia. As of 2013, the continent's population was more than 529 million.

Mexico City is the most populated city in North America. However, people also live in **remote** areas such as Nunavut, which is a territory in northern Canada.

CHAPTER SIX

INVESTIGATING SOUTH AMERICA

Most of the continent of South America lies below the equator in the Southern Hemisphere. It covers more than 6.8 million square miles (17.6 million sq km). South America is bordered by the Atlantic Ocean, the Pacific Ocean, and the Caribbean Sea. On land, there are mountains, rain forests, deserts, highlands, and plains. The Andes Mountains, the longest mountain chain in the world, run along the continent's Pacific coast. The ancient Inca people tamed this extreme environment centuries before Europeans arrived.

AUSANGATE MOUNTAIN, PERU

South America is the fourth-largest continent and contains 12 countries, including Brazil, Argentina, Chile, Peru, and Ecuador.

South America is also home to the Amazon River **basin**. It is the site of the Amazon River, the world's largest river by volume. The river begins in the Andes Mountains in Peru and drains into the Atlantic Ocean through Brazil. Freshwater dolphins, turtles, stingrays, and piranhas live in its waters.

The Amazon rain forest is in this part of South America. Many fascinating plants and animals live in the 2.3 million square miles (6 million sq km) of forests, including jaguars, poison dart frogs, spider monkeys, and macaws. These are just a few examples!

CHAPTER SEVEN

WHERE WESTERN CIVILIZATION BEGAN

Europe is bordered on three sides by the Arctic Ocean, Atlantic Ocean, and Mediterranean Sea. It shares a border with Asia. For this reason, scientists sometimes consider the joined continents as one giant landmass called Eurasia. Europe is the western part of the landmass, and it's the second smallest continent.

More than half of the land in Europe is flat, low plains. This makes the continent a good place for farming. The Alps are in south-central Europe. Plate activity deep inside the earth formed the mountain chain about 44 million years ago. The Alps are the source of many of Europe's major rivers, including the Rhône, Rhine, and Po.

TUSCANY, ITALY

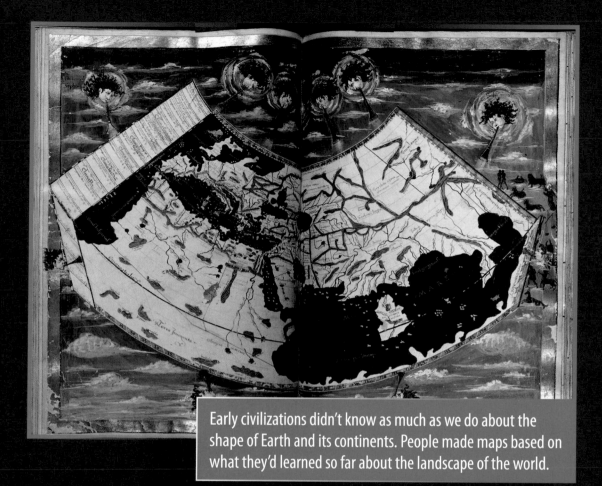

Early civilizations didn't know as much as we do about the shape of Earth and its continents. People made maps based on what they'd learned so far about the landscape of the world.

Europe's climate varies across the continent. Western Europe has a wet, **moderate** climate. Eastern Europe, which includes countries such as Poland and Ukraine, has cold winters and hot summers. Near the Mediterranean, the summers are hot and dry and the winters are mild. Europe was once covered in forests and home to large animals such as lions and bison. However, hundreds of years of human activity have made these animals all but disappear.

CHAPTER EIGHT

DOWN UNDER

Australia is a country, and it's also a continent. In fact, it's the only country that takes up an entire continent. That's how small it is!

Australia is located south of Asia, and it's surrounded by the Indian and Pacific Oceans. While it's an island today, Australia fossil **evidence** shows that it was once part of a supercontinent called Gondwana. Millions of years of plate activity caused the supercontinent to break and the pieces to drift apart. Australia probably became a completely separate landmass around 35 million years ago.

The Great Barrier Reef is off Australia's Queensland coast. It is a major geographic feature associated with Australia. The fascinating reef is home to thousands of species, or kinds, of marine plants and animals. It's like its own little world!

AUSTRALIAN OUTBACK

Australia's geography has been shaped by millions of years of erosion and weathering. Most of the continent is flat, with plateaus and lowlands covered in deserts. Australia's stretches of dry desert land are known as the outback. The outback has many kinds of landscapes, including rocky hills, plains, sand dunes, and caves. Even though it's a very dry and remote area, it is home to plentiful wildlife. Snakes, scorpions, and crocodiles are just some of the animals found there.

CHAPTER NINE

ICY ANTARCTICA

Humans didn't lay eyes on the cold, icy landscapes of Antarctica until about 1820. This continent is at the bottom of the planet, where the South Pole is. All but 2 percent of the continent's 5.5 million square miles (14.2 million sq km) is covered by an ice sheet. The ice sheet is almost 3 miles (4.8 km) thick in some areas, and holds more than half of the world's freshwater.

While Antarctica is cold today, some scientists think it was once warm. Millions of years ago, it may have been part of the Gondwana supercontinent. As it broke off and drifted south, it became cold and covered in ice. This happened over millions of years as snow that piled up in layers eventually **compacted** into ice. However, under this ice are clues about Antarctica's warm past, including fossils and coal beds.

Today, Antarctica is too cold to support much plant and animal life. Other than a few scientists, no people live there. However, plenty of fish, penguins, seals, porpoises, dolphins, and whales swim in the waters surrounding Antarctica. There is still much about this continent to discover!

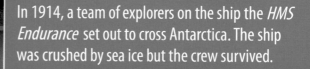

In 1914, a team of explorers on the ship the *HMS Endurance* set out to cross Antarctica. The ship was crushed by sea ice but the crew survived.

CHAPTER TEN

UNCOVERING CLUES

Most of Earth's continents were once joined as one giant landmass, but today, they couldn't be more different. From the icy landscapes of Antarctica to South America's tropical rain forests to the mountains of Asia, the continents feature landscapes, plants, animals, and people that are very **diverse**.

MESOSAUR FOSSIL

Earth scientists have spent many years discovering the secrets that the continents contain. Studying the geography and the landscapes of continents tells us a lot about the activity that happened on Earth long ago. A jagged mountain peak or a low valley are clues that glaciers once passed through an area. Fossils of the same animals found in the soils of South America and Africa are clues that these continents—today thousands of miles apart—may have once shared a border. The drifting and moving of the continents has also revealed a lot about the inside of the planet. These are amazing discoveries. What will be uncovered next?

GLOSSARY

ancestor (AN-ses-tuhr) A person who comes before others in their family tree.

basin (BAY-sin) A geographic area that is drained by a river or that drains into a lake or sea.

climate (KLY-muht) The average weather conditions in an area over a long period of time.

compacted (kahm-PAK-tuhd) Pressed together by force or pressure.

diverse (dih-VERS) Showing a great deal of variety.

environment (in-VY-run-munt) The surroundings in which a person, animal, or plant lives.

erosion (ih-RO-shun) The process of breaking down by wind, water, or other natural forces.

evidence (EH-vuh-duns) Proof that something happened.

mantle (MAN-tuhl) The partially melted layer of the earth between the crust and the core.

moderate (MAH-duh-reht) Average.

percent (per-SENT) Part of a whole.

plateau (pla-TOH) An area of relatively level high ground.

remote (rih-MOHT) Far from the main centers of population.

weathering (WEH-thuh-ring) The process of wearing away rocks and other materials by natural forces.

INDEX

PRIMARY SOURCE LIST

Page 17
World map from a 15th-century Florentine illuminated manuscript of Ptolemy's *Geographia*. Manuscript. Donnus Nicolaus Germanus, cartographer. ca. 1460-70. Now kept in the New York Public Library, Manuscripts and Archives Division.

Page 21
HMS Endurance trapped in Antarctic pack ice. Photograph. Created by Frank Hurley. 1915. Now kept in National Library of Australia digital collection.

Page 22
Mesosaurus brasiliensis fossil. Fossil. Permian Period. Now kept in Museo Civico Di Storia Naturale.

WEBSITES

Due to the changing nature of Internet links, PowerKids Press has developed an online list of websites related to the subject of this book. This site is updated regularly. Please use this link to access the list: www.powerkidslinks.com/soes/cont